W9-BXV-698

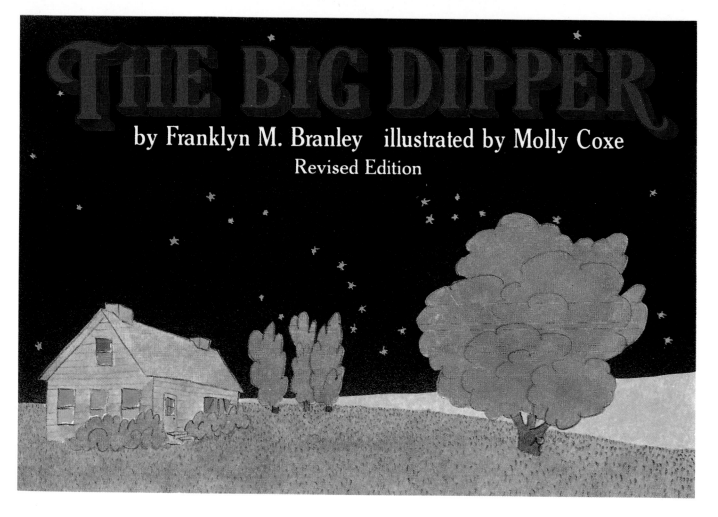

THE BIG DIPPER

by Franklyn M. Branley   illustrated by Molly Coxe

Revised Edition

HarperCollins*Publishers*

*The outlines in the illustrations for this book
were done with a black colored pencil.
The colored areas were painted in watercolor,
and an airbrush was used for the skies.*

The *Let's-Read-and-Find-Out Science Book* series was originated by Dr. Franklyn M. Branley, Astronomer Emeritus and former Chairman of the American Museum–Hayden Planetarium, and was formerly co-edited by him and Dr. Roma Gans, Professor Emeritus of Childhood Education, Teachers College, Columbia University. For a complete catalog of Let's-Read-and-Find-Out Science Books, write to HarperCollins Children's Books, a division of HarperCollins Publishers, 10 East 53rd Street, New York, NY 10022.

Let's-Read-and-Find-Out Science Book is a registered
trademark of HarperCollins Publishers

THE BIG DIPPER
Text copyright © 1962, 1991 by Franklyn M. Branley
Illustrations copyright © 1991 by Molly Coxe
All rights reserved. No part of this book may be used or reproduced in any manner whatsoever without written permission except in the case of brief quotations embodied in critical articles and reviews. Printed in the United States of America. For information address HarperCollins Children's Books, a division of HarperCollins Publishers, 10 East 53rd Street, New York, NY 10022.
1 2 3 4 5 6 7 8 9 10
Revised Edition

Library of Congress Cataloging-in-Publication Data
Branley, Franklyn Mansfield, date
  The Big Dipper / by Franklyn M. Branley ; illustrated by Molly Coxe.—Rev. ed.
    p. cm.—(Let's-read-and-find-out science book)
  Summary: Explains basic facts about the Big Dipper, including which stars make up the constellation, how its position changes in the sky, and how it points to the North Star.
  ISBN 0-06-020511-3. — ISBN 0-06-020512-1 (lib. bdg.)
  1. Ursa Major—Juvenile literature. [1. Ursa Major.
2. Constellations. 3. Stars.] I. Coxe, Molly, ill. II. Title.
III. Series.
QB802.B75 1991   90-31199
523.8′022′3—dc20   CIP
                                                          AC

THE BIG DIPPER

I like to go outside at night. Everything is still and dark. At night I can see the stars.

Some nights the stars are very bright. They look close, too. It seems that I can almost touch them. I know I cannot. They are too far away.

My father and I look at the stars. We look at them in summer and in winter. They are not always the same. In summer, these are some of the stars I see.

In winter I see these stars.

But there are some stars that I can see both in summer and in winter. I can see the Big Dipper almost every night, if the sky is clear.

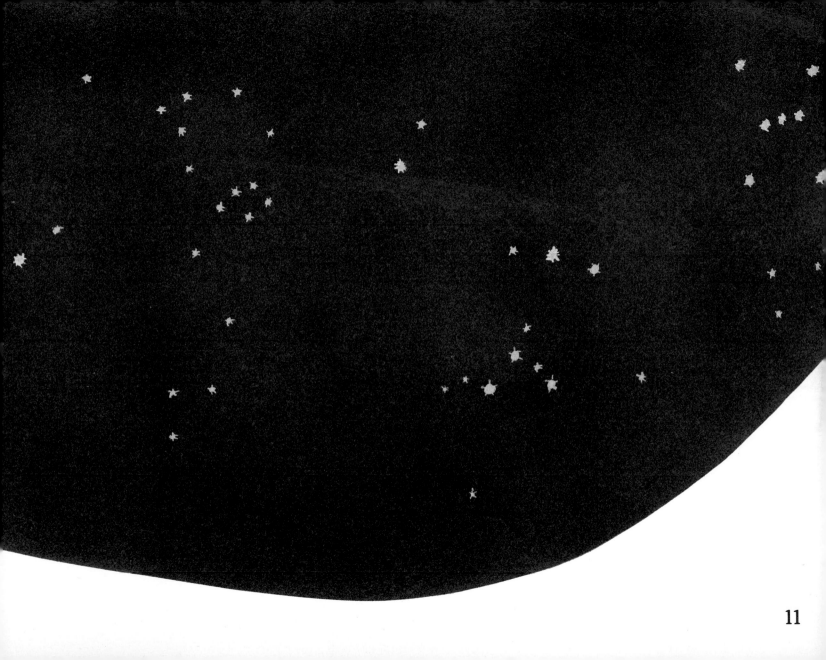

Long ago people drank water from dippers. The Dipper
in the sky looks like a water dipper. It has a bent handle,
and it has a bowl.

There are three stars in the handle of the Dipper. There are four stars in the bowl.

I use a compass to help me find the Dipper. A compass points to the north. I hold a compass in my hand. Then I look in the direction that the compass needle points.

I can see the Big Dipper in summer and in winter. On summer nights the Big Dipper looks like this.

On winter nights it looks like this.

On fall nights the Dipper looks like this. It is low in the sky. Sometimes it is so low, you may be able to see only part of it.

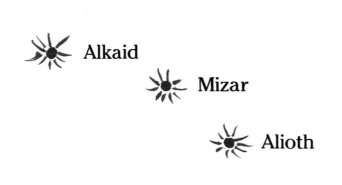 Alkaid

Mizar

 Alioth

 Megrez

 Dubhe

 Phecda

Merak

These are the names of the seven stars in the Big Dipper.
The two stars at the end of the bowl are called the pointer
stars. They point to Polaris, the North Star.

When you look at the Big Dipper in the sky, imagine a dotted line going from one star at the end of the bowl to the other one. Imagine that the dotted line goes all the way to the North Star.

The North Star is a very important star. Sailors and other travelers use it to help them find their way.

When they sail toward it, they are going north.

If they sail away from it, they are going south.

To go west, sailors keep the North Star to the right of them.

To go east, they keep the North Star to the left.

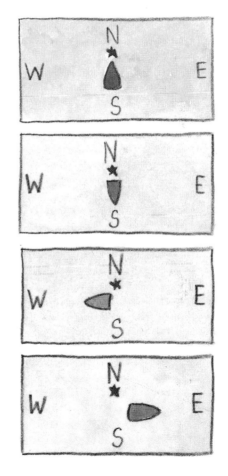

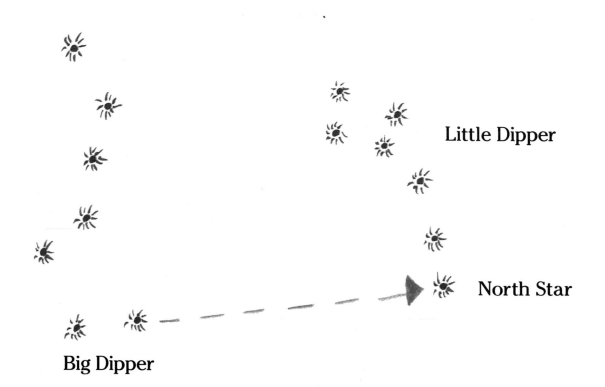

Little Dipper

North Star

Big Dipper

There is also a Little Dipper. The North Star is the first star in the handle of the Little Dipper. The Little Dipper has seven stars too. Whenever I see the Big Dipper, I can find the Little Dipper.

When the sky is clear and dark, go outside and look for the dippers. Look to the north. There you will see the Big Dipper, the North Star, and the Little Dipper.

Long ago people imagined that the Big Dipper was part of a big bear. They called it *Ursa Major*. *Ursa* means bear, and *major* means big. They imagined that the handle of the Dipper was the tail of the bear. Three pairs of stars were the paws of the bear. A bright star was his nose.

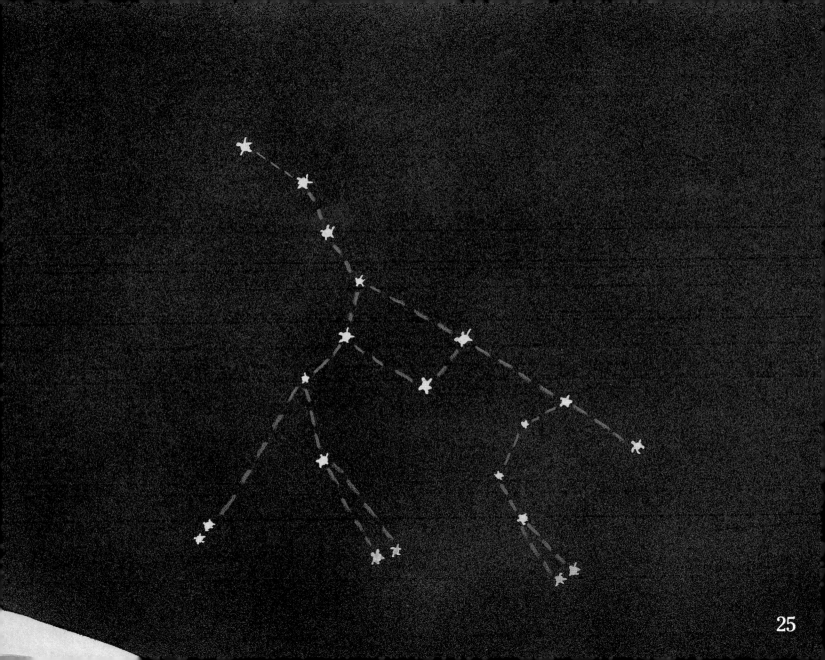

Sometimes I think I can see the tail of the bear. I make believe that I can see its head, the nose, and the four feet.

People of long ago thought that the Little Dipper was part of a little bear. Since *minor* means little, they called it *Ursa Minor*, little bear.

I try hard to imagine that I can see the little bear, but I cannot. Maybe you can.

Some night when it is still and dark, take a friend outside.
Show him how to find the Big Dipper, the Little Dipper, and
the North Star.

See if he can imagine that he sees the big bear. Maybe he'll even be able to see the little bear!